In-House(1) 0×8/16 · 4/18

6×2ⁱ

WITHDRAWN

Questions and Answers: Countries

Chile

A Question and Answer Book

by Kremena Spengler

Consultant:
Thomas A. Brown
Professor of History
Augustana College
Rock Island, Illinois

Capstone
press

Mankato, Minnesota

Fact Finders is published by Capstone Press,
151 Good Counsel Drive, P.O. Box 669, Mankato, Minnesota 56002.
www.capstonepress.com

Library of Congress Cataloging-in-Publication Data
Spengler, Kremena.
    Chile: a question and answer book/by Kremena Spengler.
    p. cm.—(Fact finders. Questions and answers. Countries)
    Includes bibliographical references and index.
    ISBN-13: 978-0-7368-3748-4 (hardcover)
    ISBN-10: 0-7368-3748-5 (hardcover)
    1. Chile—Juvenile literature. I. Title. II. Series.
F3058.5.S64 2005
983—dc22
                                            2004016451

Summary: Describes the geography, history, economy, and culture of Chile in a
question-and-answer format.

Editorial Credits
Rebecca Glaser, editor; Kia Adams, set designer; Kate Opseth, book designer; Nancy Steers,
    map illustrator; Wanda Winch, photo researcher; Scott Thoms, photo editor

Photo Credits
Art Directors/Bb Holdings, 20
Bridgeman Art Library/Index, 7
Corbis/Ludovic Maisant, 4; Tony Arruza, 27
Corel, 1
Houserstock/Dave G. Houser, cover (foreground)
Photo Courtesy of Alberto Lopez, 29 (coin, left)
Photo Courtesy of Richard Sutherland, 29 (bill)
Photo Courtesy of Worldwide Bi-Metal Collectors Club/Central Bank of Chile, 29 (coin, right)
South American Pictures/Robert Francis, 22–23; Sue Mann, 21
Stockhaus Ltd., 29 (flag)
Ulrike Welsch, 8–9, 11, 15, 17, 19
Victor Englebert, cover (background), 12–13, 25

Artistic Effects:
Ingram Publishing, 24
Photodisc/Jules Frazier, 18; Siede Preis, 16

Table of Contents

Where is Chile? 4

When did Chile become a country? 6

What type of government does Chile have? 8

What kind of housing does Chile have? 10

What are Chile's forms of transportation? 12

What are Chile's major industries? 14

What is school like in Chile? 16

What are Chile's favorite sports and games? 18

What are the traditional art forms in Chile? 20

What major holidays do people in Chile celebrate? 22

What are the traditional foods of Chile? 24

What is family life like in Chile? 26

Features

Chile Fast Facts 28

Money and Flag 29

Learn to Speak Spanish 30

Glossary 30

Internet Sites 31

Read More 31

Index 32

Where is Chile?

Chile is a long, narrow country on the west coast of South America. It is almost twice as big as California. The snowy Andes Mountains form Chile's eastern border.

Because Chile is so long, its landforms and climate change greatly from north to south. The Atacama Desert is in northern Chile. It is one of the world's driest regions. Central Chile is a valley with rich soil and mild weather. Islands, **fjords,** and glaciers form the southern tip of Chile. Heavy rain and snow fall there.

Fact!

In some parts of the Atacama Desert, it has never rained.

4

Map of Chile

Legend
- ✪ Capital
- ● City
- /// Desert
- ⛰ Mountain Range

PERU

BOLIVIA

N
W · E
S

● Antofagasta

Atacama Desert

Andes Mountains

Scale
0   250   500 Miles
0   250   500 Kilometers

PACIFIC OCEAN

Valparaiso ●   ● Viña del Mar
✪ Santiago
   Puente Alto

C H I L E

ARGENTINA

Concepción ●

Temuco ●

Andes Mountains

ATLANTIC OCEAN

● Punta Arenas

5

When did Chile become a country?

Chile became an independent country in 1818. Spain had ruled Chile since the 1500s. Chileans wanted to rule themselves. They began fighting Spain on September 18, 1810. After eight years of battles, Chile became a **republic** in 1818.

In 1970, Chile's government changed. Salvador Allende of the **Socialist Party** was elected president. His government took over many private businesses.

Fact!

Chile fought against Peru and Bolivia in the War of the Pacific (1879–1883). The three countries disagreed about natural resources in the Atacama Desert. Chile won and gained one-third more land.

In 1817, Chile won the battle of Chacabuco against Spain. It was one of many battles for independence.

In 1973, General Augusto Pinochet overthrew Allende. Pinochet had people who disagreed with him killed or arrested.

In 1988, Chileans voted to hold new elections. They chose a nonmilitary president and returned to democracy.

What type of government does Chile have?

Chile is a republic with many political parties. Usually, parties band together during elections to support candidates. Otherwise, one party cannot get enough votes by itself to win an election.

The president leads the country. He or she serves a six-year term. The president chooses advisers that make up the **cabinet**. Cabinet members help run the government.

Fact!

The president and the congress work in different cities. Congress meets in Valparaiso. The president works at the National Palace in Santiago, the capital.

Chile's congress meets in this large building in Valparaiso.

Congress makes the country's laws.
It includes the Senate and the Chamber of
Deputies. The people elect the deputies and
most senators. The president, military, and
courts choose some senators.

What kind of housing does Chile have?

Most Chileans live in apartments or houses. Rich people live in large houses with fenced-in yards. Some poor people live in pine or cardboard homes.

Many houses in Chile are built to last during the country's many earthquakes. Houses have strong concrete or brick walls.

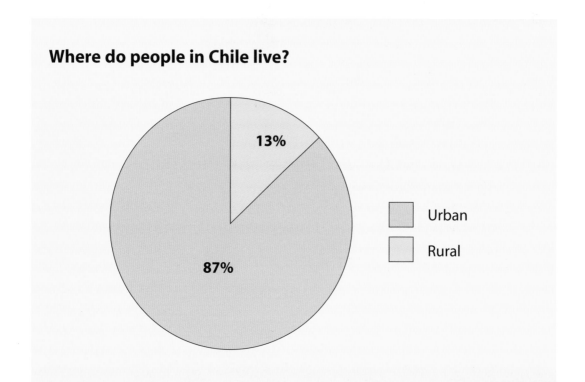

Where do people in Chile live?

13%

87%

Urban

Rural

Red tile roofs are common on houses in Chile.

Home styles in Chile differ due to the weather. In the north, little rain falls. Flat-roofed homes are common there. Farther south, it rains more often. Houses in central and southern Chile have steep roofs to help drain rainwater.

What are Chile's forms of transportation?

Chileans use both private and public transportation. They drive cars, vans, and trucks. Chile has an excellent national bus service. Many people use Santiago's modern, clean subway system.

Roads connect many places in Chile. Major highways are paved, but country roads are not. The Pan-American Highway runs the length of the country. Roads going east and west connect to it.

Fact!

Except for a detour around a rain forest in Central America, a person can drive from northern Alaska to southern Chile on the Pan-American Highway.

Cars and trucks drive on the Pan-American Highway near Santiago.

Chile's air, train, and waterway systems carry goods and people. Airplanes bridge the great distance between the north and south. Railroads lead into neighboring countries. In the far south of Chile, people travel from island to island by boat.

What are Chile's major industries?

Chile's **natural resources** have led to its large mining **industry**. The country is rich in copper, silver, and gold. The company Codelco, owned by Chile's government, is the world's largest copper business.

Fruit is one of Chile's main **exports**. It grows well in Chile's climate. Farmers grow apples, grapes, peaches, lemons, and pears.

Chile's long Pacific coast supports a large fishing industry. Fishers catch salmon, shellfish, and other ocean fish.

What does Chile import and export?	
Imports	*Exports*
cars	copper
chemicals	fish
fuels	fruit

Copper, one of Chile's exports, is refined at the El Teniente copper refinery.

Chilean factories produce many goods. Paper and other wood products are made from the country's many trees. Other factories make cloth and clothing. Machinery, equipment, and some chemicals are also made in Chile.

What is school like in Chile?

Children go to either public or private schools. Starting at age 6, students must go to school for eight years. After that, they may continue with four years of high school.

Chile has two kinds of high schools. Vocational schools prepare students for technical jobs. Art and science schools help students get ready for university programs. To go to a university, students must pass a national test.

Fact!

The school year in Chile runs from March to December. Because Chile is south of the equator, the seasons are opposite those of North America.

Two girls study during math class at a Santiago high school.

Chile does not have enough schools. Students attend school in two shifts. Some children go in the morning, and some go in the afternoon.

What are Chile's favorite sports and games?

Soccer is Chile's national game. Children learn to play soccer at a young age. Families play the game in their backyards. Chileans of all ages cheer for the national team.

Chileans ski in the Andes at world-class ski resorts. The ski season lasts from June to October.

The Lake District in south-central Chile has lakes, forests, and waterfalls. People go there for hiking, mountain biking, and white-water rafting.

Fact!

Chile won its first ever Olympic gold medal in 2004. Fernando González and Nicolas Massu won the gold in doubles tennis.

Two Chilean cowboys try to pin a steer during a rodeo.

Horses are used in some of Chile's favorite sports. Rodeo is a national sport. In Chilean rodeo, cowboys must pin a steer to a wall with their horses. At horse shows, Chilean riders show their skills. Horse racing is also popular.

What are the traditional art forms in Chile?

Chile is famous for its writers. People around the world read novels by Isabel Allende and José Donoso. Poets Gabriela Mistral and Pablo Neruda wrote about the country's beauty. Both poets received the Nobel Prize for literature.

Chile's native people, the Mapuche, are famous for their weaving.

Children in Chile enjoy dancing the cueca, *the national dance.*

The *cueca* is Chile's national dance. In this dance, a man and a woman wave handkerchiefs and imitate chickens.

Chileans also enjoy folk music. It is played with guitars and traditional instruments.

What major holidays do people in Chile celebrate?

Chileans celebrate independence on September 18 and 19. Their celebrations last for two days. During this patriotic holiday, people have parties. Parades are held around the country. People also watch rodeos.

Most Chileans are Catholic. On Christmas Eve, families go to **mass** and exchange gifts. Because Christmas is in summer, people go to the beach on Christmas Day. Catholics also celebrate Easter.

What other holidays do people in Chile celebrate?

Columbus Day
Festival of La Tirana
Labor Day
Navy Day
New Year's Day

On Domingo de Cuasimodo, priests ride in parades.

Catholics celebrate Domingo de Cuasimodo on the first Sunday after Easter. This holiday honors a historical event when priests were given protection from bandits. People decorate their homes and walk through town in parades.

What are the traditional foods of Chile?

Chilean cooking features local meats and produce. Beef and chicken stews are common. Potatoes, beans, and corn are widely used. *Humitas* is corn mashed with sugar and salt and cooked in cornhusks.

Chileans enjoy seafood. One favorite dish is eel soup with tomatoes and potatoes. Crab pudding is made with egg yolks, cheese, butter, spices, and crab meat.

Fact!

Chileans eat breakfast around 7:00 in the morning. Lunch is served around 2:00 in the afternoon. They eat a late supper around 9:00 in the evening.

A family in Valdivia prepares a lunch of steamed shellfish.

The empanada is a popular treat. This baked or fried turnover is filled with meat, cheese, or fruit.

Grapes are eaten as a dessert or used to make wine. Chile is famous for its wines.

What is family life like in Chile?

Chilean families are close. Children know their relatives well. Relatives visit each other on holidays and weekends. Most children live with their parents until they are married. People respect and care for their elderly parents.

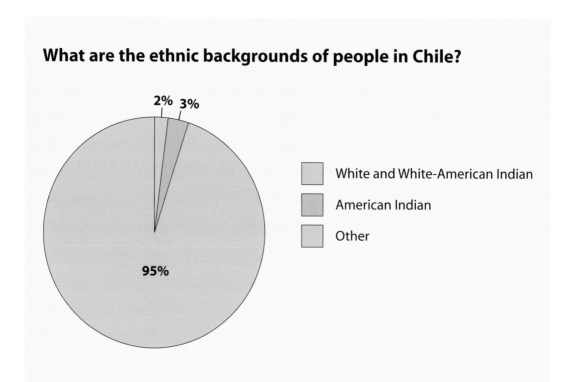

What are the ethnic backgrounds of people in Chile?

2% 3%

95%

White and White-American Indian

American Indian

Other

In Chilean farming families, everyone helps with the work.

Many Chilean mothers work outside the home in all types of jobs. Some women work as doctors, teachers, and journalists. Wealthy families hire women to do housework and care for children.

Chile Fast Facts

Official name:

Republic of Chile

Land area:

289,112 square miles
(748,800 square kilometers)

Average annual precipitation (Santiago):

15 inches (38.1 centimeters)

Average January temperature (Santiago):

68 degrees Fahrenheit
(20 degrees Celsius)

Average July temperature (Santiago):

47 degrees Fahrenheit
(8 degrees Celsius)

Population:

15,823,957 people

Capital city:

Santiago

Language:

Spanish

Natural resources:

copper, hydropower, iron ore, molybdenum, nitrates, precious metals, seafood, timber

Religions:

Roman Catholic   89%
Protestant   11%

Money and Flag

Money:

Chilean money is the peso. In 2004, 1 U.S. dollar equaled 634 pesos. One Canadian dollar equaled 479 pesos.

Flag:

The Chilean flag has two bars. The white bar stands for the snow-covered Andes. The red bar stands for people who died in the fight for independence. A blue square represents the sky. The white star stands for progress and honor.

Learn to Speak Spanish

Chile's official language is Spanish. Learn some Spanish words by using the chart below.

English	Spanish	Pronunciation
hello	hola	(OH-lah)
good morning or good day	buenos días	(BWAY-nohs DEE-ahs)
good-bye	adiós	(ah-dee-OHS)
please	por favor	(POR fah-VOR)
thank you	gracias	(GRAH-see-us)
boy	niño	(NEEN-yoh)
girl	niña	(NEEN-yah)

Glossary

cabinet (KAB-in-it)—a group of advisers for the head of government

exports (EX-ports)—goods sold to other countries

fjord (FYORD)—a long, narrow inlet of the ocean between high cliffs

industry (IN-duh-stree)—a single branch of business or trade

mass (MASS)—a Catholic worship service

natural resource (NACH-ur-uhl RE-sorss)—a material found in nature that is useful to people

republic (ree-PUHB-lik)—a government headed by a president with officials elected by the people

Socialist Party (SOH-shuh-list PAR-tee)—a political party that believes businesses and industries should be controlled by the government

Internet Sites

FactHound offers a safe, fun way to find Internet sites related to this book. All of the sites on FactHound have been researched by our staff.

Here's how:
1. Visit *www.facthound.com*
2. Type in this special code **0736837485** for age-appropriate sites. Or enter a search word related to this book for a more general search.
3. Click on the **Fetch It** button.

FactHound will fetch the best sites for you!

Read More

Crooker, Richard A. *Chile.* Modern World Nations. Philadelphia: Chelsea House, 2004.

Klingel, Cynthia Fitterer and Robert B. Noyed. *Chile.* First Reports. Minneapolis: Compass Point Books, 2002.

Kwek, Karen. *Welcome to Chile.* Welcome to My Country. Milwaukee: Gareth Stevens, 2004.

Shields, Charles J. *Chile.* Discovering South America. Philadelphia: Mason Crest, 2004.

Index

agriculture, 14, 27
Allende, Salvador, 6–7
Andes Mountains, 4, 18
art forms, 20–21
Atacama Desert, 4, 6

capital. See Santiago
climate, 4, 11, 14, 28
congress, 8, 9
copper, 14, 15

dance, 21

elections, 7, 8
ethnic groups, 26. See also Mapuche
exports, 14, 15

factories, 15
families, 18, 22, 26–27
farming. See agriculture
fishing, 14
fjords, 4
flag, 29
foods, 24–25
fruits, 14, 25

government, 6–7, 8–9, 14

holidays, 22–23, 26
housing, 10–11

imports, 14
independence, 6, 7, 22
industries, 14–15

landforms, 4
language, 28, 30

Mapuche, 20
money, 29

natural resources, 14, 28

Pan-American Highway, 12, 13
Pinochet, Augusto, 7
political parties, 6, 8
population, 10, 28
president, 6, 7, 8, 9

religions, 22–23, 28
rodeos, 19, 22

Santiago, 8, 12, 13, 28
schools, 16–17
Spain, 6, 7
sports, 18–19

transportation, 12–13

War of the Pacific, 6
weather. See climate
writers, 20